STOCK MARKET INVESTING SIMPLIFIED

A Beginner's Guide To Finding Good Stocks And Keys To Successful Investing

Bharadwaj Vanamali

ISBN 9798677122095

Contents

To my wife Anusha and my stock broker.

Chapter 1

Stock Market Investing Simplified

Stock market investing is often looked at as an enigma, especially if you are a first-time investor. You hear words like quantitative analysis and volatility thrown around and it's no wonder you want to turn around and run.

The usual investment advice that you get, especially as a beginner is either over-simplified or over-complicated. It's either so technical that the whole thing goes over your head or the usual "buy right and sit tight", which, don't get me wrong, is great advice. But how exactly do you "buy right"? That's what I've tried to answer in this book from a beginner's perspective.

Every other stock market book or blog tells you what to look for in a stock. But none of them tell you where to start.

It's not like you can analyse every publicly trading company (which in the US alone is over 3600 companies). So, how do you shortlist the stocks you would want to analyse in the first place?

Do you start with analyst recommendations or do you comb through thousands of companies and select a few for research? And if you do have that kind of time and patience, what would be your criteria for selection?

This book is my answer to those questions. In this step-by-step beginner's guide, we will look at how to evaluate and pick the right stocks without the speculation, using financial ratios.

We will be using the 'Comparables Model' to evaluate stocks based on their value and performance. As the name suggests, it compares value and performance indicators of various stocks to narrow down on companies that are relatively undervalued and efficient.

At the end of this evaluation you will have a list of stocks ranked in order of their performance and value based on financial ratios and qualitative analysis. This is the simplest and probably the most intuitive approach to stock evaluation. It can be applied to stocks in any sector or industry, trading on any stock exchange in the world.

This is unlike some of the other evaluation models that can only be used on specific company types or business models. This is why it is so popular among analysts and investors alike. So, without further ado, let's get started.

Chapter 2

A Brief Introduction To Stocks

What is a stock?

A company's stock represents a fraction or a share of the company, which is why they are also referred to as shares. Owning a company's stock essentially means that you own a part of the company proportionate to the number of shares you're holding. So, if a company issues 100 shares and you own 1 share, you essentially own 1% of the company.

Why do companies issue shares?

A company issues shares in order to raise money. Companies can raise capital through debt or equity. Debt capital is borrowed money that is to be paid at a later date with interest.

Money raised by issuing shares to investors is called equity capital. This is done by selling shares to the general public through an IPO (Initial public offering). From then on, the company becomes a publicly traded company. Subsequently the company's shares get listed on a stock exchange where they can be freely traded between sellers and buyers. It is only during the IPO stage that the issuing company is able to raise money through sale of shares. Once a stock is listed, shares are traded between individual investors without the company's involvement.

What determines the price of a share?

Just like a commodity gets its value from its limited availability, share prices are determined by supply and demand. High demand and low supply will cause the price to go up. Let's say a company's shares are sought-after by investors (buyers) because of their perceived value and at the same time existing shareholders (sellers) are unwilling to sell them at the current price. Buyers will therefore offer to pay more per share causing the share price to go up and vice versa.

In a stock exchange a company's share price is fixed as the price at which the maximum number of its shares are sold at any given time. This becomes the new market price of the share. This number keeps changing throughout the day as bids between buyers and sellers are also constantly changing.

Apart from a company's overall performance there are also other factors like press coverage, hype and market sentiment that can influence investors. This can cause stock prices to go up or down. This is why it is important to properly evaluate a stock's actual worth and not give in to herd mentality and speculation.

Chapter 3

Understanding Basic Financial Ratios

One of the most common mistakes new investors make is that they start off by investing in familiar or big-name companies, without properly evaluating them. You've probably heard the phrase "do your research" before investing. Well, this is it! This is the research part of stock market investing.

We will look at six basic metrics that can be used to determine a stock's value. Understanding these metrics and what they tell you about the stock are key to proper stock evaluation. We will later use these metrics to actually rank and pick out good, undervalued stocks from a particular sector.

The first three ratios Price to Earnings (P/E), Price to Book (P/B), Price/Earnings to Growth (PEG) as their names suggest are all price ratios, meaning that they determine whether or not a stock is reasonably priced.

Think of price ratios as a means of measuring how much bang for your buck you really get from each stock.

A high price ratio can indicate that a stock may be overpriced/overvalued. However, it can also mean that investors see value in the stock, which is why they are willing to pay higher prices for it.

On the other hand, while a low price ratio could mean that a stock may be undervalued, it can also mean that most investors do not want to pay high prices or are unwilling to buy the stock altogether. This may be because they see no value in it or because they think that the company may be in trouble.

So, looking at any single ratio in isolation can give you mixed signals about a company's worth.

This is why, as with other ratios, price ratios cannot be looked at in isolation, but rather in combination with other ratios to determine the value of a stock.

The Dividend Yield ratio is a percentage indication of a company's dividend pay-outs in relation to its share price.

The Debt to Equity (D/E) ratio is a measure of a company's financial health and its dependency on debt.

The last ratio Return on Assets (ROA) is a measure of a company's efficiency and profitability.

Let's now take a look at each of these ratios in detail.

1. The Price to Earnings Ratio (P/E Ratio)

As mentioned earlier, the price of a stock can increase for a number of reasons such as hype or positive investor sentiment. This may cause the price to temporarily rally. But what finally determines whether it will stay at that price are the company's earnings. Without earnings to justify it, the price of the stock will eventually drop once the hype dies down. The P/E ratio can be a good indicator of that.

The price to earnings ratio (P/E ratio) is the ratio of a company's share price to the company's earnings per share. It can be used to determine whether the price of a stock is high with respect to the company's earnings.

P/E ratio = Share price/Earnings per share

Let us consider two companies 'Company A' and ' Company B' both with a share price of $10.

Company A: Earnings per share = $2
              P/E ratio = 10/2 = 5

Company B: Earnings per share = $5
              P/E ratio = 10/5 = 2

For the same share price, a company with higher earnings per share has a lower P/E ratio than a company with lower earnings per share. So, in general a high P/E ratio could mean that a company's stock is overvalued with respect to its earnings whereas a low P/E ratio could mean that it is undervalued.

That's not to say that a high P/E ratio is always a bad thing. Simply put, it is an indication that investors are willing to pay more for the stock. This is because they believe that the stock will be more valuable in the future. This belief in the stock's future value could be based on any number of factors such as tangible future performance data, market hype or even positive press coverage.

Certain large cap tech stocks have high P/E ratios owing to their higher than average historic growth rates. Their high growth rate is what drives up the price. In other words, investors are willing to pay more for the stock, not because of its present earnings but because they expect earnings growth in the future. This is why a high P/E ratio can also be looked at as an indication of a company's expected earnings growth.

It is important to note that you should only compare P/E ratios of companies within the same or similar sector (i.e. compare a tech stock with another tech stock). This is because the average P/E ratio is different for different sectors. This will give you an idea of whether that hot stock pick that everyone is talking about is actually worth the premium at which it is trading or if you should wait for its price to come down.

To sum up:
1. A low P/E ratio could indicate that the stock is undervalued (i.e. relatively cheap).
2. A high P/E ratio could mean that a stock is overvalued (i.e. relatively expensive).
3. A high P/E ratio could also mean that investors strongly believe in the company's future growth and are willing to pay more for the stock.
4. P/E ratios are different for different sectors, only compare companies within similar sectors.

2. The Price to Book Ratio (P/B Ratio)

A company's book value is the value of all the company's physical assets (factories, buildings, land, equipment, etc.) minus it's liabilities like loans and other financial obligations. The price to book ratio of a company is the ratio of the share price to the book value per share of the company. In other words, it is the measure of a company's worth without its earnings.

P/B ratio = Share price/Book value per share

Book value = Assets – Liabilities

Book value per share = Book value/Total number of shares

Some companies such as financial firms may have highly fluctuating P/B ratios since they are predominantly made up of financial assets like cash, stocks or bonds rather than capital assets like buildings and land. Furthermore, some companies with little to no physical assets such as gaming companies can have a very low book value. Such companies tend to have higher P/B ratios.

So once again it is important that you only compare P/B ratios of companies within similar sectors or industries. It is also advisable to only compare companies operating within the same country. This is because accounting practices vary from country to country which may affect the book value calculation. This will in turn affect the final P/B ratios used for comparison.

A low P/B ratio is generally regarded as a good sign and the stock is considered to be undervalued. In some cases, the P/B ratio may even be less than one, indicating that the stock price is less that the value of the company's assets per share. This means that even if the company were to go bankrupt, it can sell all its assets and investors can still make a profit. However, in a few cases, it can also be a sign that there is something wrong with the company, which may be why it is priced so low.

This is why, as with the other metrics, the P/B ratio should not be looked at by itself but in combination with other ratios and metrics to evaluate a stock. Many investors have used P/B ratios to discover dormant stocks that eventually went on to become very valuable.

To sum up:
1. A low P/B ratio is generally a good sign signifying a relatively high book value (assets minus liabilities) and an undervalued stock.
2. A high P/B ratio could mean that a stock is overvalued and has high levels of debt (but not always).
3. Some businesses like gaming companies which have very little physical assets have a lower book value when compared to say auto manufacturing companies, which are more capital and equipment intensive.
4. Such companies with lower book values may have low P/B ratios which doesn't necessarily mean that the stock is overvalued or that the company is in trouble.
5. P/B ratios are different for different sectors, only compare companies within similar sectors.

3. The Price/Earnings to Growth Ratio (PEG Ratio)

The PEG ratio can be considered to be a more comprehensive version of the P/E ratio since it also takes a company's expected future earnings into account. Looking at a high P/E ratio by itself may give you an indication that a stock may be overvalued. However, the high price may be justified by its expected earnings growth.

PEG ratio = P/E ratio / Earnings growth rate

Company A: P/E ratio = 5
                Earnings growth rate = 10%
                PEG ratio = 5/10 = 0.5

Company B: P/E ratio = 2
                Earnings growth rate = 1%
                PEG ratio = 2/1 = 2

In the above example, 'Company A' has a higher P/E ratio than 'Company B'. This may initially give you an indication that it may be overpriced. But as you can see, Company A's high earnings growth justifies its price. This is signified by its low PEG ratio. This is why the PEG ratio is a more balanced indicator of a stock's value. It can be used as a litmus test to see if a stock's true value justifies its high price.

It is important to check the data used to calculate the PEG ratio. For e.g. If historic earnings growth figures are used, the ratio may be inaccurate. This is because the company's future earnings may differ from past earnings. Just like the other ratios, PEG ratios must only be compared between companies withing similar industries or sectors. In theory a PEG ratio of less than 1 means that a stock is undervalued, equal to 1 means it is fairly valued and greater than 1 means it is overvalued.

To sum up:
1. A low PEG ratio could indicate that a stock is undervalued.
2. A high PEG ratio could indicate that a stock is over-valued.
3. PEG ratios are different for different sectors, only compare companies within similar sectors.

4. Debt to Equity Ratio (D/E Ratio)

The debt to equity ratio is the measure of a company's debt/liabilities (loans, mortgages, unpaid expenses, etc.) vs the value of a company's assets after paying its liabilities. In other words, the D/E ratio is a measure of the company's financial health and its dependency on borrowed capital. It can be looked at as the ability of a company to meet its financial obligations.

It is the ratio of a company's total liabilities to its total shareholder's equity. Shareholder's equity is the total assets a company owns minus its liabilities.

D/E Ratio = Total liabilities/ Shareholder's Equity

Shareholder's equity = Assets - Liabilities

As far as an investor is concerned, the lower the D/E ratio the lower the company's risk of loan defaults or bankruptcy. Although the benchmark D/E ratio varies from industry to industry, general consensus is that a D/E ratio between 1 and 1.5 is acceptable. Anything higher than 2 may be cause for concern.

However, some capital-intensive industries like telecom or oil may have D/E ratios higher than 2, which is normal. This is why it is important to only compare companies within the same industry.

To sum up:
1. A low D/E ratio is generally a good sign, indicating that a company has low levels of debt and has good financial health.
2. A high D/E ratio means that a company has a higher dependency on borrowed capital, thereby increasing the risk of loan defaults or bankruptcy.
3. However some capital-intensive industries like telecom or oil generally tend to have higher D/E ratios when compared to other sectors, which may not

necessarily be a bad thing.

4. D/E ratios are different for different sectors, compare companies within similar sectors.

5. Dividend Yield

Dividends are pay-outs issued by a company as a reward to its investors for trusting and investing in its shares. Dividends are usually paid out annually or quarterly and sometimes even intermittently when a substantial profit is made. Dividend yield is the percentage of dividend paid out by a company relative to its stock price.

Dividend Yield = (Dividend per share/Share price) x 100

For eg: Apple's Dividend per share = $3.27
            Apple's share price = $364.11

Dividend Yield = (3.27 / 364.11) x 100 = 0.90%

Dividend yield by itself need not be looked at as a sign of a good stock. Some companies which have been around longer may pay higher dividends when compared to new ones. Newer companies tend to reinvest their profits into the company to promote growth rather than distribute it to investors. Dividend pay-outs also vary from industry to industry.

Although dividends can be a bonus in addition to the appreciation of the stock itself, they need not be your sole criterion when picking a stock. However, irregular or decreasing dividend pay outs may be warning signs of a company's failing financial health.

To sum up:
1. Dividends are like rewards paid out by companies to their investors for investing in their shares.
2. Companies that have been around for longer generally pay higher dividends when compared to newer companies.
3. Newer companies tend to re-invest profits into their business rather than issue dividends.
4. Although Dividend Yield can be a good source of additional income from shares, it should not be your sole criterion for stock selection.

6. Return on Assets (ROA)

Return on Assets (ROA) is an indication of how efficiently a company uses the money and resources available to it to generate profits. It is the ratio of a company's net operating income to it's total assets.

ROA % = (Net Income/ Total Assets) x 100

Net Income = Earnings - (Interest + Tax + Expenses)
ROA gives you a much better understanding of a company's profitability rather than just looking at its

profit margins. For e.g. Take two companies with profit margins of 10% and 15%. Looking at the profit margins alone may give you the idea that the second company is more efficient. But if it uses double the amount of capital as the first company to generate that profit, it is actually less efficient. This is where ROA succeeds in gauging a company's efficiency.

To sum up:
1. ROA measures how efficiently a company uses its resources and capital to generate profits.
2. The higher the ROA, the more efficient a company is in using its capital to generate profits.

Yay! You now have a basic understanding of the six metrics that we will be using as screening criteria for our stocks. The first five give you an idea of a stock's value (over/undervalued). The last metric (ROA) can be used to gauge the company's performance and profitability. When used in combination you can compare stocks to gauge their relative valuation.

Although there are numerous other ratios that evaluate a company's liquidity (current ratio, quick ratio, etc) and operating efficiency (ROE, ROCE etc), from a beginner's perspective, the six ratios discussed here should give you a fairly good picture of a company's health and the stock's value.

Chapter 4

Choosing A Market Cap

Before we can move on to ranking our stocks, we must first decide on a market-cap to choose our stocks from. The market capitalization or market-cap of a company is its total number of outstanding shares times the value of each share. For e.g. If a company has issued 1 million shares priced at $10 each, then it's market-cap would be $10 million. Depending on their market-cap, companies are classified into mega, large, mid and small-cap companies.

Companies smaller than small-cap are classified into micro and nano cap categories which we will not go into detail about, since they are considerably high-risk investments when compared to other market caps. Nano cap stocks are also referred to as penny stocks.

Although the cut-off ranges used in classifying stocks as large, mid or small-cap can vary from country to country, the principle remains the same.

Mega-cap companies have a market capitalization of over $200 billion. These are some of the largest companies in the world. They are usually front runners in their respective industries. Out of all the market caps, mega-cap companies are considered to be least risky and most stable. Their dividend pay-outs are generally the highest among all the market caps. Owing to their large size, they have the least growth potential and are best suited for long term investing. Due to the abundance of data and market research available, it is relatively easier to gauge and evaluate such companies. Apple, Amazon, Microsoft and Facebook are a few examples of mega cap companies.

Large-cap companies are those with a market-capitalization between $10 billion and $200 billion. These are well-established companies and are generally more stable in terms of profitability and revenue generation and are considered safer investments when compared to mid and small-cap companies. They usually pay out higher dividends to their investors when compared to companies with smaller market caps. Although less risky, large-cap companies have a lesser growth potential when compared to mid and small-cap companies.

Mid-cap companies are companies with a market-cap between $2 to $10 billion. Mid-cap stocks are considered to be riskier investments because they are more volatile (i.e. prone to greater price fluctuations with changing market conditions) when compared to mega and large-cap stocks. Their dividend pay-outs are also understandably lesser than large-cap companies. However, they are considered to have a higher potential for growth and increase in profits when compared to large-cap companies.

Small-cap companies have a market-cap between $250 million and $2 billion. Although they have a very high growth potential, they are considerably riskier investments when compared to their mid and large-cap counterparts. This is because most of them are just starting out and have little to no track record to put any real trust in. Small cap companies generally get their notoriety from the associated fraud and lack of transparency, but then again so do large and mid-cap companies from time to time. They are also subject to a greater degree of volatility when compared to the other two categories. It is important to note that some of the most successful companies of today started their journey as small-cap stocks.

I personally would not recommend starting off with small-cap stocks till you gain experience. This is because of the high risk associated and the difficulty involved in stock evaluation due to insufficient historic data. Start off with mega-cap stocks till you are confident enough to move on to smaller market caps. That said, choose a market-cap based on your risk appetite.

Chapter 5

Quantitative Analysis (The Ranking System)

DIY Stock Analysis: Identifying and Choosing The Right Stocks

We will now use the six metrics we looked at earlier to actually rank stocks from a particular sector. You can choose from a variety of free as well as paid stock screeners to get these metrics. TradingView and Yahoo Finance are some of the free stock screeners you can use for screening and filtering global stocks. I will be using Finviz (which is a free screener for US stocks) for this demonstration because it is very beginner friendly.

Since the aforementioned metrics are best suited to compare stocks within the same industry/sector, we will start out with a particular sector and then go about finding our top-ranking stocks within that sector.

1. Let's start off the screening process by selecting a sector (say 'technology') to choose stocks from.

2. Now choose the desired market cap (Mega, Large, Mid or small) using the market cap filter.

3. After this, go to the custom tab, click on settings (top right corner). Here you can choose the metrics that you would like to use to analyse the stocks.

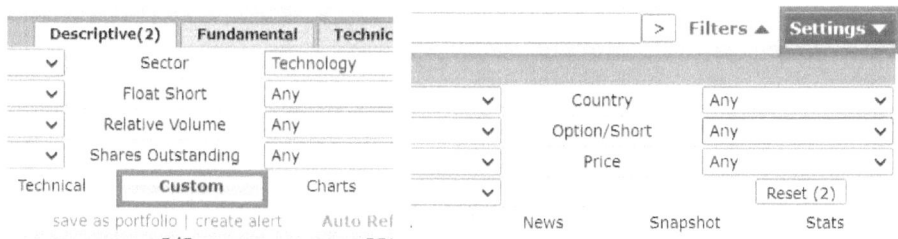

4. Deselect the default checkboxes except for the 'No.', 'Ticker' and 'Company' checkboxes. Select the 'Market Cap', 'P/E', 'PEG', 'P/B', 'Total Debt/Equity', 'Dividend yield' and 'ROA' checkboxes.

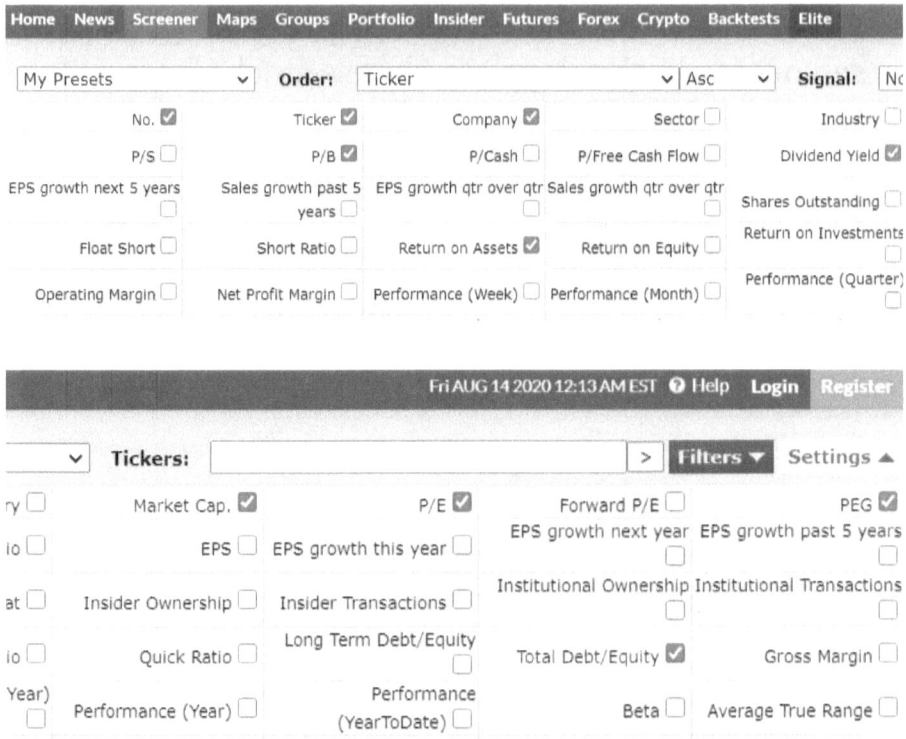

5. The list of stocks along with the metrics you selected will now appear in the table below in alphabetical order.

6. Toggle the 'Market cap' column to display the stocks in a descending (high to low) order of market cap. This is indicated by a downward pointing triangle next to the 'Market cap' column heading.

7. You can now choose the desired number of stocks from the list for evaluation (say the first 50 to 100 stocks).

Note: Remember, the stocks on the list are in the order of high to low market-cap and not necessarily in the order of high to low value. By evaluating more stocks your comparative analysis will yield more comprehensive results. If you choose a limited number of stocks for analysis, say the first 10 or 20, you may very well be missing out on some good stocks that may not have made it to your list.

8. Enter the stocks you've selected for evaluation along with their respective metrics into a spreadsheet as shown in the screenshot below. You can use Microsoft Excel or other similar software.

STOCK	P/E RATIO	RANK 1	PEG RATIO	RANK 2	P/B RATIO	RANK 3	D/E RATIO	RANK 4	DIVIDEND YIELD	RANK 5	ROA	RANK 6	RANK 1+2+3+4+5+6
Company A	10.5	4	9.5	4	8.8	4	0.5	2	5.4	1	13.5	2	17
Company B	7.8	3	4.3	2	4.3	3	0.32	1	3.2	2	10.4	3	14
Company C	2.4	1	6.2	3	2.1	2	0.9	3	2.1	3	6.4	4	16
Company D	4.3	2	2.5	1	1.5	1	1.2	4	1.7	4	18.4	1	13

USE 'SUM' FORMULA

ENTER MANUALLY

USE 'RANK' FORMULA

9. The hard part is manually entering each individual ratio for every stock into the spreadsheet. Once you manage to do that, we can use the 'RANK' function in Excel to automatically rank each metric. On my first try, it took me around 55 minutes to rank 100 stocks.

Now, I know this may seem like a tedious task but hear me out. As I mentioned earlier, every other stock market book or article tells you what to look for in a stock. But none of them tell you where to start.

It would be impractical to analyse every publicly trading company just to pick out good stocks. So, how do you decide which stocks you would want to analyse in the first place?

This method, in my opinion, is the only sensible way in which you can arrive at top-ranking stocks in a particular sector, on your own, without wracking your brains.

Put simply, it is a way of shortlisting stocks by ranking them based on their value and performance, which you can then choose from for further scrutiny.

Now that we've addressed that, let's continue our evaluation.

Note: There may be some financial data missing for a few stocks on the screener. This usually either means that a company is new or that the particular ratio is negative. Negative ratios are usually not a good thing. Either way, for the sake of convenience, omit all the stocks which have missing ratios from your list (except for dividend yield, a missing dividend yield can be assumed to be zero).

10. The first four metrics: P/E, PEG, P/B and D/E ratios must be ranked in ascending order (i.e. low to high) using the Ascending 'Rank' function. For e.g. If you are evaluating 50 stocks, the stock with the lowest P/E ratio gets rank 1 and the one with the highest P/E ratio gets rank 50. Do the same for the PEG, P/B and D/E ratios.

To learn how to use the Excel 'Rank' function, watch the "*How To Rank Items Using Excel RANK Functions*" video on YouTube (between 1:06 and 3:01). It's fairly simple to follow. Here's the link to the video:

https://www.youtube.com/watch?v=Qqkjkt3VBPs

11. The last two metrics: Dividend Yield and ROA must be ranked in descending order (i.e. high to low) using the descending 'Rank' function. So, the stock with the highest Dividend yield gets rank 1 and the stock with the lowest dividend yield gets the last rank. Do the same for the ROA column.

12. Once each ratio is ranked, add up all the individual ranks for each stock to get a 'Final rank'. You can use the 'Sum' function to do this.

END .D	RANK 5	ROA	RANK 6	RANK 1+2+3+4+5+6	
4	1	13.5	2	17	LOWEST RANKED STOCK
2	2	10.4	3	14	
1	3	6.4	4	16	
7	4	18.4	1	13	HIGHEST RANKED STOCK

The stock with the least 'Final rank' figure is your highest ranked stock and the one with the highest 'Final rank' figure is your lowest ranked stock.

So, what we've basically done is separately rank each stock from best to worst based on individual ratios. We've then added the individual ranks to get an overall rank for each stock based on all the ratios. You now have a list of stocks for a particular sector, ranked in order of their value and company profitability to choose from. This is known as quantitative analysis.

You can choose the top 4 or 5 stocks from your list for further qualitative analysis. This process can be applied to stocks from any sector (e.g. finance, healthcare, etc.) to find undervalued stocks from each sector.

Note: The companies identified from this evaluation should NOT be looked at as stock picks for investment without further research or consulting a financial advisor. The point of this exercise was to help you understand the basics of stock analysis and serve as a starting point to identifying undervalued stocks and efficient companies.

Chapter 6

Qualitative analysis
Assessing a company's sustainability

Using quantitative analysis, we have narrowed down to our top stock picks by evaluating and comparing companies from a particular sector.

Having done that, we must also examine each company's long-term sustainability by taking a closer look at its management and its competitive advantages before making our final stock pick. This is known as qualitative analysis since it is somewhat subjective and cannot be quantified using ratios or percentages.

A Competent and Trustworthy Top-Level Management

Good management is key to the efficient operation of a company. The top-level management (CEOs,

Executives) of a company is typically responsible for taking key financial and operational decisions and keeping the company on course. This is why it is important to ensure that the people at the helm know what they are doing and that they have the best interest of their shareholders in mind.

Look for stocks that have consistently been good performers. A good long-term stock performance is usually regarded as a sign of good management.

The management's interests should be in line with the shareholder's interests. Identify companies with a high promoter's stake, the higher the better. This way the promoter has incentive to ensure that the stock performs well. A steady increase in the promoter's shareholding is also a good sign of the company's confidence in its own stock.

Another thing to check is how long the CEO and top-level executives have been with the company. Longer tenures signify a company's ability to retain top level management which is ultimately a sign of stability. This also means a more experienced management at the wheel that is in tune with the industry and the inner workings of the company.

And last but not least, make sure that the management and top-level executives are qualified and have a clean track record. Check to see if they have been involved in scams or fraudulent practices of any kind. Look at their credentials and employment history. A quick google search should give you all the information you need.

A Strong Economic Moat

Invest in companies with a strong economic moat. Popularized by Warren Buffet, a company's economic moat is its ability to maintain a competitive edge over its contenders in the industry. It gets its name from castle moats which served as the first line of defence against intruders in medieval times.

A company's moat can be its brand value, cheaper access to raw materials, patents, network effect and so on. Essentially it is the things that cannot be easily replicated by a competitor, thereby ensuring the company's sustainability and its ability to maintain its market standing in the long term.

Amazon is a perfect example of a network effect moat. It recognized that building its network of suppliers and customers would mean it could demand lower prices. More sellers also mean a wider variety of products thereby attracting more customers. In turn more customers mean more sellers willing to use Amazon to sell their products.

In the case of Google, it's the company's sheer scale, intellectual property and brand value that give it a competitive advantage over other contenders in the industry. Due to Google's popularity, more websites and services would like to rank on google searches to get found. This further increases its popularity among users thereby improving its ad targeting capability.

Using qualitative analysis, you can single out companies with a sound management and a strong economic moat from your list of top stocks. In doing so you are ensuring that your final stock picks have a definite advantage over their competition and that they will most likely stand the test of time.

Congratulations! You now have a basic understanding of how to identify stable and financially efficient companies with relatively undervalued stocks using financial ratios and qualitative analysis. As mentioned earlier this is ideal for shortlisting stocks within a particular sector or industry.

Although there are numerous other ratios and evaluation models you can use for stock evaluation, from a beginner's perspective, the one's we looked at can serve as a good introduction to understanding stock analysis.

As mentioned earlier, the companies identified from this evaluation should NOT be looked at as stock picks for investment without further research and evaluation or without consulting a financial advisor first.

You can compare your results with buy/sell recommendations from professional analysts or sites like Zacks, Yahoo finance, Simplywall.st, etc.

However, analyst recommendations should be taken with a grain of salt. While one may have a 'buy' rating, the other may have a 'sell' rating on the same stock.

Recommendations can vary depending on the types of firms the analyst works for or based on how they are compensated. For e.g. An analyst working for a mutual fund would most likely have 'buy' ratings on stocks that the fund is holding and 'sell' ratings on the stocks the fund has already sold (which is not necessarily a bad thing).

So, although analyst recommendations can be used as a reference when picking stocks, they should not be your sole criterion for stock selection.

Chapter 7

10 Keys To Successful Investing

A common misconception is that you need to be a financial whiz with years of experience in order to become a successful investor. The most important qualities a successful investor must possess are common sense, patience and the ability to resist blindly following the crowd (herd mentality).

That said, there are a few basic principles that every investor should follow in order to succeed in their investing journey. These principles are not just applicable to stock market investing, but can be applied to investing in general. So, without further ado, here are 10 keys to successful investing.

1. Start Investing Early
2. Invest Regularly
3. Think Long-Term
4. Diversify Your Investments

5. Asset Allocation
6. Re-Balance Your Portfolio Regularly
7. Don't Try To Time The Market
8. Monitor Investments Regularly
9. Avoid Panic Selling
10. Turn Adversity Into Opportunity

1. Start Investing Early: Greater Risk Appetite

In the investment world, high gains are generally synonymous with high risk. It is the investments with higher volatility and a greater potential for capital loss that generally yield higher returns in the long run.

Depending on an investor's age and risk appetite, his/her investment decisions boil down to one of two choices: wealth creation or wealth preservation.

For a young investor the main priority is wealth creation. His/her primary objective would be to build up savings and create a large enough retirement corpus. This is known as the accumulation phase of investing. On the other hand, an older investor nearing retirement would be more concerned about preserving the wealth he/she has worked so hard to create over the years.

With the majority of their earning years ahead of them, young investors can afford to take greater risks and invest in more aggressive investments in pursuit of higher returns. Compared to older investors, they will be in a better position to cope with capital loss or short-term volatility.

Stocks, mutual funds and equity related investments in general fall in the high-moderate risk category, whereas debt related assets and pension schemes are considered to be low risk.

2. Invest Regularly: Dollar Cost Averaging

Investing regularly not only instils the habit of saving and curbs overspending but also gives you the added benefit of dollar cost averaging. As investors, one of our primary aims is to acquire an asset when it is relatively cheaper.

However, this is easier said than done. Due to constant fluctuations in price, it is difficult for even the most well-versed investor to accurately time purchases each time.

Dollar cost averaging takes the thinking out of the equation. By investing a fixed amount regularly, say every month, irrespective of the price of the asset, you are ensuring that the cost of the asset averages itself out over a period (say 1 year), rather than investing a lump sum.

For e.g. Let's say you've decided to invest $12,000 in a stock. Instead of investing a lump sum amount, you decide to invest $1000 per month over a one-year period. Like any other asset, the share price will go through its fair share of fluctuations throughout the year.

Month	Share Price	Shares Purchased
January	16	62
February	17	58
March	12	85
April	14	71
May	9	112
June	20	50
July	4	250
August	6	166
September	18	55
October	14	72
November	11	91
December	10	100

Total Amount Invested $= \$11995$

Average Share Price $= \$10.23$

Total Shares Purchased $= 1172$

As you can see in the above example, despite the monthly fluctuations in price, your average purchase price of each

44

share will have been $10.23 and the total number of shares purchased will have been 1172 with $5 to spare out of the $12000.

Notice that because our monthly investment was a fixed amount (around $1000), it led to the purchase of a smaller number of shares when prices were high and more when prices were low. For e.g. 250 shares were purchased in July when the share price was lowest ($4) as opposed to only 50 shares purchased in June when the share price was highest ($20). So, the lower the price, the more shares purchased and vice versa.

This means that most of your shares are purchased at the lowest possible market price ensuring good value for your money. This form of automatic regulation is another advantage of investing a fixed amount regularly.

Now in contrast, let's say instead of investing regularly you decided to invest a lump sum amount of $12000 at the beginning of the year. At $16 per share you would have been able to buy only 750 shares as opposed to the 1172 shares you could get through regular investments.

Of course, one can argue that if purchased at $4 per share in July, you would've been able to buy 3,000 shares. But since none of us can time the market that accurately without speculation, regular investments are the easiest way to ensure good value for money.

So, to summarize, investing fixed amounts regularly not only curbs over-spending but also ensures that you benefit from dollar cost averaging.

3. Think Long-Term

Apart from the obvious benefit of compounding, long-term investing also reduces investment risk and volatility experienced in the short-term. Volatility is the fluctuation in the price of an invested asset. Long-term investing is also a tax efficient investment approach.

Reduced Risk/Volatility

Assets that are generally considered volatile in the short term such as stocks and other forms of equity investments not only have the potential to deliver higher returns but also become less volatile over
a longer time period.

There may be ups and downs in the short term, but what is important is the general trend of an asset. Take a look at the S&P 500 stock index for example. Although there

are peaks and valleys over a monthly or even a yearly time frame, when considering a longer period, the general trend is an upward rise.

Stress-Free Investing

Long-term investing is also a lot less stressful when compared to short-term investing. This is because you don't have to worry about timing your investments when markets are low or get anxious about selling when markets are booming.

Once you've decided to stay invested for the long term, short-term uncertainties and volatility will not seem as worrisome.

Tax Efficiency

Tax efficiency is another advantage of long-term investing. Assets such as stocks, mutual funds, real estate and gold are generally taxed less when held for a longer period (over one year). This is known as long-term capital gains tax.

For e.g. Stocks held for over one year are taxed at 0, 15 or 20% depending on your taxable income and filing status.

If held for less than a year, gains from these assets will be added to your taxable income and taxed as per your tax slab usually at a higher tax percentage. This is why it pays to stay invested for longer.

4. Diversify Your Investments

Diversification is another key aspect of successful investing. As the old saying goes, "Don't put all your eggs in one basket".

Diversification not only results in lower risk but also in higher overall returns. This is because not all asset classes are equal. Varying market conditions affect different types of investments differently.

Take stocks and gold for example. In terms of performance they are inversely related to each other, which means that when one is under performing, the other almost always performs well.

Whenever there is an economic crisis and stock markets are under-performing, people tend to shift away from equity related assets towards gold and gold related investments for stability. This results in a rise in gold prices causing gold related investments to perform well, while almost everything else is under performing.

So, the advantage of diversification is that at any given time, when one asset class in your portfolio may be under-performing, another asset class may be performing well, since it is not affected by the present market condition.

Diversification also ensures that your portfolio has a good balance of low-risk and high-risk investments. For instance, if you're portfolio predominantly consists of high-risk investments, although there is a potential for higher returns, there is also a risk of loss of capital or under performance.

Similarly, if an investor is too conservative and invests only in low-risk assets, he/she may not be able to reach their financial goals due to poor returns.

Diversification is therefore essential to reduce the overall volatility of a portfolio and strike a balance between risk and returns.

5. Asset Allocation

As the name suggests asset allocation is the distribution of funds among various asset classes such as equity, debt, etc. In other words, it is deciding the percentage of your money you are willing to invest in each asset class.

Asset allocation should be done after carefully considering the investor's long and short-term financial goals, age and risk-appetite.

As discussed earlier, a younger investor can afford to park a large portion of their assets in relatively high-risk investments such as stocks and mutual funds in pursuit of higher returns. On the other hand, an investor nearing retirement may have to adopt a more conservative investment strategy.

In order to accumulate wealth, young investors have to invest a little more aggressively so as to generate enough returns to build a corpus.

For an older investor, protecting the wealth already earned will be a bigger priority than creating and accumulating wealth, since the majority of their earning years are behind them, making it more difficult to cope with volatility or capital loss.

That said, even the most conservative investor's portfolio should have at least a small percentage of aggressive investments in the form of blue-chip stocks or mutual funds in order to generate returns and beat inflation.

As a general rule of thumb, it is advisable to follow the '100 minus present age' rule, according to which your asset allocation in equity (i.e. stocks/mutual funds) should be equal to 100 minus your age. So, if you are a 30-year-old, the equity allocation in your portfolio must be 100 – 30 = 70% and the remaining 30% can be invested in debt instruments such as government bonds, debt mutual funds, etc.

This percentage will keep changing every year, thereby ensuring that you slowly shift towards safer investments as your age progresses.

Asset allocation should also ensure enough liquidity (the ability to convert an asset into cash) for any short-term requirements or emergencies, which is why it is important to review lock-in periods, early withdrawal penalties and tax implications when allocating assets.

6. Re-balance Your Portfolio Regularly

Portfolio re-balancing is the process of periodically re-distributing your investments in order to maintain your target asset allocation. It prevents the portfolio from being overexposed to any one particular asset, thereby bringing the risk down to an acceptable level as originally intended.

Let's say your portfolio's value is $100,000, with an asset allocation of 75/25 i.e. 75 % ($75,000) in equity and 25 % ($25,000) in debt investments (such as government bonds, debt mutual funds, etc).

Now let's assume that your equity investments alone have increased in value to $100,000 while debt investments have grown to $28,000 taking your portfolio's total value to $128,000. Asset allocation is no longer 75/25. Equity allocation has increased to 78% while debt investments have reduced to 22%. Since your investment percentage in equity is more than you originally intended, you are exposed to a greater risk.

Although it may seem sensible to stay invested in a better performing asset, this would put your portfolio at a greater risk than originally intended.

In order to bring the portfolio back to its original asset allocation of 75/25, you would have to cash out a proportionate amount of equity investments and re-invest into debt, thereby restoring the original balance. This is why it is known as portfolio re-balancing.

Another advantage of re-balancing is that by selling an asset that is performing well and investing in a relatively under performing asset, you are essentially selling high and buying low.

Although there are several re-balancing strategies, the one that is most commonly used and requires no active monitoring is 'Calendar re-balancing'.

Calendar re-balancing involves reviewing and re-adjusting your portfolio at specific intervals in order to maintain your target asset allocation. It is generally recommended that you re-balance your portfolio at least once every year to ensure that your investments stay on track.

7. Don't Try To Time The Market

Trust me when I tell you that when it comes to timing the market, many have tried and failed. According to a 2018 study, between 1992 and 2014, 63 countries across the world experienced a total of 153 recessions, of which economists were only successful in predicting 5.

What makes it so difficult is that all markets are ultimately governed by the interaction between buyers and sellers, who at the end of the day are human after all, humans driven by fear and greed, who are easily swayed by hype and misinformation.

So, no matter how well you think you've analysed the market, human behaviour is almost impossible to predict. This is why, rather than trying to time the market, try to analyse the asset. In other words, instead of trying to choose the right time, try to pick the right investments through good research and analysis.

Timing the market can also be a stressful exercise, since it requires constant monitoring. Even when an asset falls down to your target price range for purchase, many a time, greed kicks in, pushing you to wait till it falls further.

While all this is happening, you are effectively losing out on potential gains as you wait for the perfect time. Furthermore, frequent buying and selling decisions will also cost you in the form of transaction fees and taxes.

This is why trying to time the market can be a very costly and time-consuming affair, one with a very poor track record for success.

Instead, make regular, long-term investments so as to benefit from dollar cost averaging and a reduced overall volatility.

8.Monitor Investments Regularly

Although long term investing means that you don't tinker with your investments often, it doesn't mean you shouldn't monitor them regularly. Monitoring your

investments from time to time gives you a good indication of how efficient your investment strategy is and how effectively it is being implemented. After all, your ultimate aim is to build wealth.

It is important to review your portfolio from time to time in order to identify investments that may not be performing as well as expected. Frequent monitoring will also tell you if you need to re-balance your portfolio or adjust it so that you steadily move towards less aggressive investments as you age.

Make a Financial Plan

In order to track the performance of your investments, it is important that you have a financial plan in place. A financial plan can be used to establish your long-term and short-term goals and put strategies in place to achieve those goals. It serves as a benchmark to monitor your investments.

For instance, you first need to determine how much retirement corpus you would require, in order to decide the type of investments you should opt for. Depending on the figure you arrive at and based on your estimated monthly expenses and additional income sources, you can go about establishing investment strategies to reach your goals.

If you find that you are falling short of your goals, you can compensate either by investing more aggressively i.e. invest in assets with a higher risk profile or increase your monthly/annual investment amounts.

Once you establish clear-cut financial goals, you can then go about planning your investment strategy around it.

9. Avoid Panic Selling

Whenever there is a dip in the markets or a global economic crisis looming, you are bound to see a lot of investors who quickly try to cash out all their investments in an attempt to minimize their losses. While this may seem like a sensible thing to do, most of the time it isn't.

Fear causes a lot of people to act irrationally during market downturns causing them to sell at a loss. In fact, this panic selling drives stock prices down even further.

By panic selling when your portfolio is down, you are selling low and actually making the losses real. By staying calm and remaining invested it will merely be a temporary dip in your portfolio till the markets recover (provided you invested in a good underlying asset after thorough market research in the first place).

As an investor you have one of three options during times like this:

1. Give in to herd-mentality and sell, out of panic, thereby making your losses real.
2. Remain calm and ride out the downturn, so that your losses remain temporary and hypothetical (provided you did your research and picked fundamentally good stocks in the first place).
3. Use the downturn as an opportunity and pick up assets available at a discount, so as to realize high gains in the future.

If you have the money and don't require it in the short-term, my personal favourite is Option No: 3, which is what we will delve deeper into next.

10. Turn Adversity Into Opportunity

Although every economic downturn may seem like the end of the world, they are a fairly common, unavoidable aspect of any investor's journey. Thankfully bear markets are much shorter than bull markets. A bear market is where most stocks are declining in value due to an economic crisis

So, instead of giving in to panic and speculation, you can use down markets as an opportunity to identify undervalued assets for investments.

Invest In Undervalued Stocks

Bear markets are one of the very few times when fundamentally good stocks are available at a discount. However, it is important to properly analyse and identify undervalued companies with a good track record, before considering investing.

Almost everything is available at a discount in bear markets. Make sure you identify good stocks through thorough research, if and when you decide to invest.

Note: Do not break your existing investments for re-investment. When you cash out on underperforming assets you are essentially selling low. Only use surplus funds available for investment.

Take Refuge In Alternate Assets

Gold is a classic example of an asset class that has historically performed exceptionally well when conventional assets such as stocks and mutual funds were under performing.

This is because during times of economic uncertainty, people tend to shift to gold for investment for its stability and as a hedge against inflation. So, essentially gold performance is inversely proportional to the stock markets i.e. when stock markets are down, the demand for and subsequently the price of gold goes up.

However, even if you decide to invest or increase your asset allocation in gold, it should not exceed 10% of your portfolio's value.

Epilogue

First of all, thank you for buying my book out of the fairly large selection available. I sincerely hope that it was of some use to you. If nothing else I hope it was at least successful in demystifying the basic principles of stock analysis and investing. Please take a minute to review the book and let me know what you thought about it.

My main objective with this book was to simplify some of the basic aspects of stock analysis and explain the logic behind various investment strategies. I've tried to refrain from using financial jargon except where unavoidable.

I strongly believe that you don't have to be a financial genius in order to understand stock market investing or become a successful investor. If I can do it, so can you. As I had mentioned earlier, all you need is some common sense, a little bit of discipline and a whole lot of patience.

I would like to end the book with a quote that highlights the importance of maintaining individuality and not giving in to herd mentality when it comes to investing. Because what book about stock markets would be complete without a Warren Buffet quote? (and a disclaimer, there's definitely going to be a disclaimer at the end).

"The most important quality for an investor is temperament, not intellect. You need a temperament that neither derives great pleasure from being with the crowd or against the crowd."

– Warren Buffet

About The Author
Bharadwaj Vanamali

Hi there!

Hope you enjoyed the book. Let me start off by saying that I'm just an average investor like you. Ok, maybe slightly above average :) Ever since I bought my first stock at 21 years old, I've tried my hand at everything ranging from oil futures to cryptocurrencies.

Trust me when I tell you that I've made some huge mistakes in the past and bet some pretty large sums on questionable investment strategies. Although foolish in retrospect, they've helped me gain practical, first-hand experience over the years, making me the investor I am today.

Let's look at it this way, I've made all the mistakes on your behalf, so you don't have to.

Of all the other forms of investment, stocks are my favourite. They have afforded me the financial freedom to pursue the things I love, that I otherwise wouldn't have been able to.

My aim is to share my experience in investing by letting you know what works and what doesn't in as simple a manner as I possibly can.

Most often, anything related to finance is looked at with apprehension and can be anxiety-inducing for a lot of us. This is because we fear what we don't fully understand.

I'd like to change that by simplifying financial education, making it easy to understand and accessible to everyone.

Hope to see you soon in another book. Until then, Happy Investing!

Disclaimer

The information provided in this book is for informational purposes only and is not intended to be a source of advice or credit analysis with respect to the material presented. The information and/or documents contained in this book do not constitute legal or financial advice and should never be used without first consulting with a financial professional to determine what may be best for your individual needs.

The publisher and the author do not make any guarantee or other promise as to any results that may be obtained from using the content of this book. You should never make any investment decision without first consulting with your own financial advisor and conducting your own research and due diligence.

To the maximum extent permitted by law, the publisher and the author disclaim any and all liability in the event any information, commentary, analysis, opinions, advice and/or recommendations contained in this book prove to be inaccurate, incomplete or unreliable, or result in any investment or other losses.

Content contained or made available through this book is not intended to and does not constitute legal advice or investment advice and no attorney-client relationship is formed. The publisher and the author are providing this book and its contents on an "as is" basis. Your use of the information in this book is at your own risk.

The stock evaluation detailed in this book in no way eliminates the possibility of some of the top ranked stocks under-performing or some of the low-ranking stocks performing better than expected. There are exceptions to every rule, especially in the stock market. At the end of the day, there's no real way to predict how a company will perform in the future. The best anyone can do is take an educated guess which is what this method of relative analysis aims to do using past performance and indicators of expected growth.

Any stock screener/screeners detailed in this book have been used for demonstration purposes only and should not be considered as recommendations for use. Stock screeners use databases that update on different schedules. Always check the relevance and timeliness of the data. Before investing, the user must check the correctness of the data at their own end. Due to the nature and speed of information, there is no guarantee that the information is accurate, complete or up-to-date.

Past performance is not necessarily indicative of future performance.

There is a substantial risk of loss associated with trading these markets. Losses can and will occur.

No representation or implication is being made that using the methodologies or systems or the information contained within this book will generate profits or ensure freedom from losses.

Examples presented here are not solicitations to buy or sell. The author, publisher and all affiliates assume no responsibility for your trading results.

There is a high risk in stock market investing and trading.

www.ingramcontent.com/pod-product-compliance
Lightning Source LLC
Chambersburg PA
CBHW020619220526
45463CB00006B/2629